AI for Educators & Trainers

Create, Personalize & Scale Learning

By Joe Correa

Published by Live Stronger Faster

First Edition

Table of Contents

Introduction

Artificial Intelligence has already transformed the way we work, communicate, and build businesses—but one of its most profound impacts is unfolding quietly in classrooms, lecture halls, and digital learning platforms across the world. The education system, which for centuries relied on standardized lessons and one-size-fits-all teaching methods, is being rewritten by intelligent algorithms capable of personalizing learning for every student. For educators, coaches, and trainers, this is not just an evolution—it's a revolution. AI is now the most powerful teaching assistant, curriculum designer, and classroom analyst ever created. And it's ready to help you teach, train, and inspire at a level that was once unimaginable.

Today's learners expect more than passive lectures or static slides—they crave interactive, adaptive, and personalized experiences. Whether you're teaching in a school, coaching professionals online, or creating your own courses for global audiences, AI can help you deliver education that meets every learner where they are. Imagine instantly generating quizzes that adjust to a student's performance, chatbots that act as 24/7 teaching assistants, or entire video lessons produced automatically from a text outline. With tools like ChatGPT, Scribe, Synthesia, Quizgecko, and other AI-powered platforms, you can design full courses in hours instead of weeks. The once-overwhelming task of lesson planning, content creation, grading, and student engagement can now be streamlined into one intelligent, automated system—freeing you to focus on what truly matters: connection, creativity, and impact.

AI doesn't replace teachers. It empowers them. It doesn't eliminate the human touch in learning; it enhances it by handling repetitive tasks and providing real-time feedback. As a result, educators can spend more time mentoring, inspiring, and creating transformative learning experiences. For private tutors and course creators, AI unlocks scale. You can now reach thousands of students simultaneously, offering each one a customized journey through your material. Whether you teach financial literacy, language learning, fitness, or software development, AI allows you to create "smart courses" that learn from your students as they learn from you.

One of the greatest promises of AI in education lies in **personalization**. No two learners absorb information the same way—some are visual thinkers, others prefer step-by-step logic, and some thrive on interaction and gamification. Traditional teaching models simply can't accommodate all these differences at scale. But with AI, personalization is automatic. Machine learning systems can track a student's pace, weaknesses, and preferences to adjust lesson difficulty and content type in real time. What was once a manual process of trial and error is now an intelligent feedback loop that improves every session. The result? Faster learning, higher retention, and a level of engagement that feels like a private tutor for every student.

But the transformation doesn't stop in classrooms. Corporate trainers, coaches, and consultants are now using AI to elevate their learning programs too. Through automation tools, they can onboard new clients, test knowledge with AI-generated quizzes, and send automated progress reports. Instructors can instantly generate lesson transcripts, summaries, and highlight reels using video AI platforms. They can use ChatGPT to script their lessons, Midjourney or Leonardo AI to generate images and slides, and ElevenLabs to narrate them in multiple voices and languages. With these tools, even a solo educator can operate like a global academy. The barrier to entry for building scalable education businesses has been permanently lowered—and those who embrace this change early will thrive.

Still, as with every revolution, there are challenges. The rise of AI in education brings important ethical questions about bias, accuracy, and the role of human creativity. It also requires teachers to learn new digital skills and adapt their methods to hybrid and virtual environments. But the good news is that AI itself can help you learn how to use it. By integrating these technologies step by step—starting with lesson design, then moving to quizzes, grading, and automation—you can evolve at your own pace while reaping the benefits almost immediately.

This book is your complete roadmap to doing exactly that. In the chapters ahead, you'll discover how to use AI to:

- Plan entire curriculums, courses, and workshops using smart prompts and frameworks.
- Generate engaging multimedia lessons—video, voice, and slides—without complex tools.
- Build personalized learning paths that adapt to your students' progress automatically.
- Use AI analytics to measure engagement, comprehension, and retention.
- Automate grading, feedback, and communication while maintaining a personal touch.
- Expand your reach with multilingual AI narration and translation tools.
- Turn your expertise into scalable online courses that generate recurring income.

Each concept in this book is designed not just to inform but to transform. You'll see real-world examples of educators and trainers who have already integrated AI into their teaching—individuals who went from local classrooms to global audiences, from time-consuming lesson prep to automated learning systems that run 24/7. You'll learn how to replicate their success, step by step, using accessible tools and workflows.

By the end of this book, you'll understand that AI isn't just changing how people learn—it's changing who can teach. The power to educate is no longer limited to schools or large organizations. It belongs to anyone with knowledge, passion, and a message to share. Whether you're a teacher, coach, entrepreneur, or subject-matter expert, AI can help you become a world-class educator capable of transforming thousands of lives.

The future of learning is intelligent, interactive, and infinitely scalable—and it begins here, with you.

Chapter 1: The New Era of Teaching: How AI Transforms Education

The world of education has reached a turning point unlike any in history. For centuries, the model of teaching was fixed: a single instructor delivering information to a group of students, regardless of their pace, preferences, or unique learning needs. This system worked when access to information was scarce and learning resources were limited to physical classrooms and textbooks. But in today's hyperconnected digital world—where knowledge multiplies faster than we can absorb it—traditional teaching methods can no longer keep up. Artificial Intelligence (AI) is emerging as the most powerful tool to revolutionize how we teach, learn, and design education systems.

At its core, AI in education means using algorithms and intelligent tools to automate repetitive tasks, analyze learning data, and personalize instruction. Teachers and trainers spend countless hours creating materials, grading, tracking progress, and trying to engage students. AI removes much of this friction by generating lessons, quizzes, and summaries automatically. It can assess student performance in real time, identify weak points, and adjust lessons instantly. For the first time, educators can offer the kind of one-on-one attention that was once only possible in small tutoring settings—but now at global scale.

One of the most profound transformations AI brings is **adaptive learning**. Traditional education assumes that students of similar age or level learn at the same pace. AI proves this wrong. Using machine learning, adaptive systems analyze how each student interacts with materials—what they get right, where they struggle, and how long they take—and then tailor content accordingly. For example, if a student consistently struggles with fractions, an AI-powered platform can automatically provide additional explanations, step-by-step examples, and even switch teaching methods (such as visual or gamified lessons) until mastery is achieved. This personalization ensures no student is left behind, and high performers can accelerate instead of waiting for others to catch up.

Equally powerful is AI's ability to help **educators create faster and teach smarter**. In the past, designing a course required weeks of preparation, writing scripts, recording videos, and designing slides. With tools like ChatGPT, you can now draft full lesson plans in minutes. Platforms such as Synthesia and HeyGen generate video lessons with AI avatars that speak your scripts in natural voices. Quizgecko and ClassPoint can create interactive quizzes automatically from your notes or textbooks. Even grading can be automated through AI-based evaluation systems that assess open-ended responses with remarkable accuracy. This doesn't replace the teacher's judgment—it enhances it, allowing educators to focus on human connection, mentorship, and creativity.

AI also democratizes education by **removing barriers of geography and language**. In the past, a teacher's reach was confined to a classroom or, at best, a local audience. Now, AI translation and voice cloning tools allow you to reach students across the world. Platforms like ElevenLabs and Whisper AI make it possible to instantly translate, dub, and narrate lessons into multiple languages with your own cloned voice. A teacher in Florida can teach financial literacy to students in India, Brazil, or Germany—without ever learning another language or recording multiple versions of the same course. This global reach empowers educators to scale their impact beyond borders.

Another emerging trend is **AI-driven learning analytics**. Modern platforms can monitor engagement levels, quiz accuracy, video watch times, and even emotional tone (through webcam analysis or feedback patterns). This data helps teachers adjust their methods and content dynamically. For instance, if 70% of students pause a video at a certain minute, the system may alert the instructor that something is unclear. If students frequently skip a topic, it might suggest a restructured sequence or shorter explanation. Data that once required manual surveys or guesswork is now instantly visible through visual dashboards. This is the foundation of data-driven teaching—a world where feedback is continuous and actionable.

However, successful AI integration requires understanding the **balance between automation and authenticity**. AI can generate lessons, but it cannot replace human empathy or intuition. The most effective educators will be those who combine technology with humanity—who use AI as a collaborator, not a replacement. While AI handles structure and repetition, the teacher provides mentorship, emotional intelligence, and inspiration. Education will increasingly rely on this synergy: intelligent machines that deliver precision and efficiency, guided by compassionate humans who bring purpose and meaning.

For trainers, coaches, and course creators, AI also opens the door to **profitable scalability**. You can now record one intelligent course that adapts itself to each learner. Imagine a fitness coach whose AI assistant tracks client progress and adjusts routines automatically, or a language teacher whose virtual tutor provides 24/7 pronunciation feedback. These systems allow professionals to teach thousands without sacrificing quality. Combined with online platforms like Kajabi, Teachable, or Udemy, AI-powered teaching becomes not just educational—but entrepreneurial. The next decade will redefine the meaning of being an educator. Teachers will evolve into "learning designers," guiding students through personalized journeys built with AI tools. Textbooks will transform into living, adaptive experiences. And classrooms will extend into virtual spaces accessible from anywhere. AI will not only teach facts; it will teach *how to learn*—a skill far more important for the uncertain world ahead.

In this new age of intelligent education, knowledge is no longer limited by time, space, or traditional systems. Anyone with expertise and a vision to teach can now build a global classroom. Whether you're an elementary teacher, a corporate trainer, or a course entrepreneur, the opportunity is the same: to use AI as your most powerful ally in shaping the minds of tomorrow. The sooner you start experimenting with these tools, the faster you'll discover the joy of teaching in ways that are smarter, faster, and more human than ever before.

"The Classroom Without Walls"

When Maria Alvarez walked into her classroom that morning, she didn't realize it would be the day her teaching career changed forever. For nearly twenty years, she had been teaching English at a public school in Texas. She loved her students—the laughter, the curiosity, the sense of purpose that came with helping them find their voices. But she also carried the exhaustion that came with endless grading, lesson planning, and trying to keep every student engaged at once. Her days stretched long past sunset, her weekends disappeared into stacks of papers, and still, she felt she wasn't reaching everyone the way she wanted. Some students thrived. Others silently fell behind.

One afternoon, during a professional development seminar, a speaker demonstrated an AI-powered learning platform that could generate personalized reading exercises for each student. The system tracked vocabulary retention, sentence comprehension, and writing fluency—all in real time. Maria was skeptical. She had seen plenty of tech fads come and go. But something about this was different. The AI didn't just automate—it *adapted.* It seemed to understand each student like an invisible co-teacher.

She decided to try it. Over the next few weeks, Maria uploaded her reading materials into the platform, then assigned her students digital lessons. To her surprise, the system created individual learning paths within seconds. One student who struggled with grammar received simplified examples and practice sentences; another, who excelled, was given more complex challenges. The AI even provided feedback on tone, sentence rhythm, and creativity—areas Maria never had enough time to analyze deeply.

Within a month, her classroom felt transformed. The students were more engaged than ever before. The quietest ones began participating because the AI tutor had built their confidence through small wins. The strongest students weren't bored anymore—they were motivated by new challenges. Maria spent less time managing logistics and more time connecting emotionally, mentoring, and storytelling. For the first time, she felt like she was teaching *humans*, not managing a process.

One afternoon, she stayed after class to review the AI analytics dashboard. It showed detailed insights she had never imagined possible: how long students spent reading, which words confused them, and where they needed emotional encouragement. She realized that data wasn't cold—it was empathy in numbers. The AI wasn't replacing her; it was amplifying her reach. She could finally see her students not as a class, but as individuals.

Encouraged by the results, Maria went further. She recorded short video lessons using an AI avatar that spoke in her voice but with perfect clarity and timing. She translated her materials into Spanish and Portuguese using ElevenLabs, reaching students abroad who began messaging her on social media, thanking her for making English accessible. One student from Brazil wrote, "Your class changed my life. I finally feel like I can speak with confidence." Months later, Maria's story went viral in educator circles. She was invited to host online workshops for teachers worldwide, showing them how to blend AI with compassion. She called her approach "The Classroom Without Walls." What started as a local experiment had grown into a global movement. She no longer spent nights grading papers; instead, she mentored teachers from five continents.

As Maria watched her students graduate, she realized she hadn't just improved test scores—she had unlocked something far greater: the freedom to teach with purpose again. AI hadn't taken her job; it had given her back her time, her creativity, and her connection to learning itself. Standing before her final class of the year, she looked at the smiling faces and said softly, "Remember—AI is not here to replace you. It's here to remind you that your voice, your curiosity, and your story still matter. Technology teaches facts. We teach people."

And with that, Maria turned off the projector, smiled, and walked out of her classroom into a world where education had no walls—only endless possibilities.

Chapter 2: AI-Powered Course Creation & Curriculum Design

Curriculum design has always been both an art and a science. Teachers dedicate countless hours developing lesson plans, aligning objectives with standards, selecting materials, and ensuring lessons reach every student. Yet, despite all this effort, traditional curriculum design often falls short of meeting the diverse needs of students in a modern classroom. Enter Artificial Intelligence—a revolutionary force that transforms how educators create, organize, and deliver learning content. AI doesn't just help teachers plan faster; it helps them plan *smarter*.

AI-powered curriculum design begins with one fundamental shift: **from standardization to personalization**. In the past, teachers were forced to design one version of a lesson that fit an entire class. But with AI tools, educators can create dynamic, flexible curricula that adapt to individual learning levels, interests, and progress. Imagine planning a semester of history lessons where each student receives a version tailored to their reading comprehension, attention span, and curiosity. A student fascinated by military strategy can receive case studies on ancient battles, while another interested in culture explores art, language, and daily life—all from the same unit.

This is not science fiction; this is what adaptive learning engines powered by AI now make possible.

Teachers can use AI systems like **ChatGPT**, **Eduaide.AI**, or **Curipod** to design entire lesson sequences aligned with academic standards. These tools generate objectives, activities, and assessments that fit specific grade levels and subjects. For instance, by typing "Create a 4-week 8th-grade biology unit on ecosystems aligned with NGSS standards," a teacher can instantly receive a complete framework: lesson outlines, group activities, lab ideas, and formative assessments. The teacher's role then shifts from manual creation to refinement—evaluating, editing, and enhancing AI-generated plans with their professional judgment and creativity. This not only saves time but also enhances quality, ensuring lessons are coherent, varied, and engaging.

AI can also be used to **generate differentiated materials** automatically. For decades, teachers have struggled to provide multiple versions of the same material for students at varying reading levels. With AI text simplifiers and expanders, a single lesson can now exist in multiple forms: simplified text for English language learners, extended explanations for advanced students, and culturally contextual examples for diverse classrooms. Tools like **Diffit**, **MagicSchool AI**, and **Explainpaper** help teachers transform any passage into a version that meets each learner where they are—without additional manual labor. This empowers teachers to give every student equitable access to content.

Another major advancement is AI's ability to **visualize complex subjects**. Educators no longer need to search endlessly for the right diagrams or multimedia examples. AI image generators like **Bing Image Creator**, **Canva Magic Studio**, and **Midjourney** allow teachers to instantly create visual aids, historical reconstructions, and interactive maps. A science teacher can generate an image of the water cycle customized for middle schoolers, or a geography teacher can create a 3D-style map for a specific region. These visuals increase retention and make abstract topics come alive, improving comprehension and engagement.

Beyond visual learning, AI now plays a central role in **course pacing and evaluation**. Intelligent scheduling tools analyze the complexity of a subject and the time available, suggesting how to structure lessons for maximum retention. AI learning analytics can also flag when a class is collectively struggling with a topic—alerting teachers to reteach or adjust materials. This level of precision brings the concept of "teaching to mastery" within every educator's reach.

A particularly exciting innovation is **AI-assisted**

cross-disciplinary design. Teachers can collaborate with AI to create lessons that merge multiple subjects, helping students understand how knowledge connects in the real world. A history and literature teacher might co-create a unit where students study the Industrial Revolution through both historical documents and literary works. AI tools can align objectives, design shared rubrics, and even suggest joint assessments. The result is more integrated, meaningful learning experiences.

For administrators, AI streamlines curriculum alignment and compliance. School leaders can use AI dashboards to ensure every teacher's lessons meet required standards, track progress across grades, and identify resource gaps. Instead of manual audits, AI can generate visual reports showing coverage of learning outcomes and highlight areas needing improvement. This not only saves administrative time but also improves educational quality and consistency across departments.

Perhaps the most transformative impact of AI in curriculum design is how it **frees teachers to focus on creativity and mentorship**. Instead of starting from scratch, educators begin with AI-generated blueprints and then enrich them with real-world stories, local relevance, and human warmth. This shift moves teachers from content creators to *learning* *architects*—professionals who guide AI to shape environments where curiosity thrives. The teacher's value becomes not the repetition of facts, but the creation of connection, critical thinking, and imagination.

However, effective AI integration requires digital literacy and ethical awareness. Teachers must learn how to evaluate AI outputs, verify accuracy, and guard against bias. AI can occasionally misrepresent facts or generate content that lacks cultural sensitivity, so it's essential to review and adapt materials before implementation. Training programs that teach educators prompt design, AI ethics, and digital creativity will be key to maximizing AI's benefits.

Ultimately, AI-powered course creation represents the future of teaching: faster preparation, deeper personalization, and higher engagement. Schools that embrace these tools will not only save time but also elevate learning outcomes. Teachers will no longer feel overwhelmed by endless planning but inspired by endless possibility. AI is not here to replace lesson plans—it's here to give them life, adaptability, and purpose. The next chapter in education begins not with fear, but with creativity—and teachers guiding AI will be the authors of that future.

"The School That Redesigned Itself"

The first time Principal Raymond Hughes heard about using AI for curriculum design, he almost laughed. His school—Lincoln Middle, a small district in Ohio—had limited funding, outdated textbooks, and teachers who already felt overworked. The idea that artificial intelligence could somehow fix these issues felt like a fantasy. "We don't need robots," one veteran teacher had said. "We need more time." But when a nearby district introduced an AI tool called MagicSchool that helped teachers plan entire units in minutes, Hughes decided to take a closer look.

He began small. Two teachers volunteered to pilot the system: Ms. Patel, a seventh-grade science teacher, and Mr. Donovan, an English instructor. Both had spent years juggling lesson planning, grading, and extracurricular duties. They were skeptical, but open-minded. Hughes gave them one month to experiment with the new platform.

In the first week, Ms. Patel uploaded her old lesson plans into the AI system. Within seconds, it reorganized them into clear modules aligned with state standards. It suggested new interactive experiments and visual simulations she'd never thought of before. It even broke down each topic into differentiated reading levels, offering alternate materials for struggling students. "I felt like I suddenly had a team of assistants," she told Hughes. Meanwhile, Mr. Donovan used the same tool to turn his poetry unit into an interactive, multimedia experience. The AI generated creative writing prompts, short quizzes, and even a visual poetry analysis guide.

Within two weeks, something remarkable happened. Students began noticing the change. They were more engaged, asking better questions, and submitting assignments faster. The lessons didn't just feel modern—they felt alive. Parents emailed the teachers to say their kids were talking about school at the dinner table again. The classrooms buzzed with energy that had been missing for years.

Hughes decided to expand the program. By mid-semester, nearly every teacher was using AI in some capacity. The math department created adaptive quizzes that automatically adjusted difficulty. The social studies teachers used AI to simulate historical debates—students could ask AI "characters" from the past about their decisions. Art and language teachers collaborated to design interdisciplinary projects, mixing visual storytelling with creative writing. The school was no longer just teaching content; it was creating experiences.

But the biggest surprise came from the teachers themselves. Instead of fearing AI, they began embracing it. The hours once spent crafting worksheets or rewriting rubrics were now invested in creativity and mentorship. Ms. Patel started a lunchtime "Science Lab Club," while Mr. Donovan launched a podcast featuring student poetry readings. The school's culture shifted from burnout to inspiration. By the end of the school year, Lincoln Middle's standardized test scores rose by 18%. More importantly, attendance improved, and student surveys reflected newfound enthusiasm for learning. Hughes presented the results to the school board with tears in his eyes. "We didn't just adopt new technology," he said. "We rediscovered why we teach."

The district soon received media attention, calling Lincoln Middle "The School That Redesigned Itself." Other principals visited to observe the transformation. When asked what made it work, Hughes always gave the same answer: "It wasn't the AI alone—it was the teachers who learned to dance with it."

One quiet afternoon, as Hughes walked the halls, he passed a classroom where a group of students was debating climate change policies using AI-generated research summaries. Their discussion was rich, informed, and passionate. He realized that what they were learning went far beyond facts—they were learning how to think.

That night, he wrote in his journal: *The machines didn't take over our classrooms. They gave them back to us.*

Chapter 3: AI-Powered Assessment, Grading & Feedback Systems

Assessment is one of the most essential yet time-consuming aspects of education. For decades, teachers have relied on tests, essays, and class participation to evaluate student learning. Yet, traditional grading methods often lack consistency, scalability, and immediate feedback. Artificial Intelligence has introduced a new era of assessment—one that is continuous, adaptive, and data-driven. By leveraging machine learning and natural language processing (NLP), educators can now evaluate not only what students know but *how* they learn, think, and apply knowledge.

The conventional approach to grading—collecting assignments, scoring manually, and providing written comments—has long placed significant administrative pressure on teachers. A 2021 RAND Corporation study found that the average educator spends nearly **10 hours per week** on grading and feedback alone. This workload limits opportunities for creative instruction and individualized attention. AI systems change this dynamic by automating repetitive grading tasks while preserving teacher oversight. Platforms like **Gradescope**, **Turnitin Draft Coach**, and **ChatGPT-integrated rubrics** can instantly analyze written assignments, detect plagiarism, and suggest grade ranges based on preset criteria. These systems don't just save time—they improve fairness and consistency by minimizing subjective bias.

AI also redefines *assessment design.* Instead of single, summative tests, educators can now implement **formative assessments** that evolve throughout a course. Adaptive testing platforms like **Century Tech**, **Quizizz AI**, and **Knewton Alta** analyze a student's real-time performance and modify the next question's difficulty based on previous answers. This personalized approach aligns with research in cognitive psychology showing that *spaced repetition* and *incremental difficulty* enhance long-term retention. In other words, AI assessments learn about learners as they learn.

Beyond multiple-choice grading, AI excels in analyzing **open-ended responses**, long essays, and even creative projects. NLP algorithms can evaluate sentence structure, argument strength, coherence, and vocabulary diversity. Tools such as **ETS's e-Rater**, used in standardized exams like the GRE, and **OpenAI's text analytics models** can detect logic, flow, and tone in written work with remarkable precision. While human review remains essential for nuanced interpretation, AI provides a foundational assessment layer that reduces time without sacrificing accuracy. Teachers can then focus on qualitative feedback—guiding students on creativity, originality, and deeper understanding.

Feedback, historically delayed by days or weeks, is now immediate. This is one of the most powerful pedagogical shifts AI brings. Students learn best when feedback is *timely, specific,* and *actionable.* AI platforms can now generate personalized comments within seconds of submission. For instance, an AI tool might tell a student, "Your thesis is clear, but your supporting examples could be stronger. Consider adding evidence from paragraph two to reinforce your argument." This form of dynamic feedback encourages *iterative learning*, where students improve progressively rather than waiting for end-of-term evaluations.

Equally important, AI can help teachers understand *how students think* through **learning analytics dashboards**. These dashboards visualize engagement metrics—such as time on task, revision frequency, and cognitive load—offering insights previously unavailable through traditional grading. Schools that integrate AI analytics gain a comprehensive picture of student development, helping identify struggling learners early and adjust instruction accordingly. A 2023 meta-analysis in the *Journal of Educational Computing Research* found that classrooms using AI-based feedback systems saw an average **30% increase in student**

self-efficacy and **24% improvement in retention** compared to control groups.

AI grading systems also bring greater **transparency and equity**. Traditional grading can be influenced by unconscious biases—handwriting, tone, or even cultural references. AI, when trained ethically and monitored carefully, can minimize these biases by assessing purely on content quality and alignment with learning objectives. However, it's vital to note that bias can still exist if the AI model itself was trained on unrepresentative data. This makes *ethical AI deployment* essential in schools, requiring periodic calibration and teacher oversight.

In addition to text-based assessments, AI is expanding into **multimodal evaluation**. Computer vision tools like **Proctorio** or **GoReact AI** can assess oral presentations, body language, or lab demonstrations by analyzing facial expressions, voice modulation, and confidence indicators. This approach allows educators to evaluate not just cognitive understanding but *communication skills*—a key predictor of real-world success. AI can also support language teachers by analyzing pronunciation accuracy and fluency through speech recognition.

Despite its transformative potential, integrating AI into assessment requires new digital competencies among educators. Teachers must understand how to interpret AI-generated results, correct errors, and contextualize findings within human judgment. Professional development programs in "AI literacy for educators" are crucial for this transition. Research from UNESCO's 2024 *Education Futures Report* emphasized that schools implementing AI without proper teacher training risked reducing assessment quality due to over-reliance on automation. Therefore, a hybrid model—where AI handles data and educators handle interpretation—remains the most effective.

The ultimate goal of AI-powered assessment is not to replace grading but to **make learning measurable in richer, more meaningful ways**. By continuously analyzing data, AI transforms grades from static numbers into living indicators of growth. Students begin to view assessment not as judgment but as feedback for mastery. Teachers reclaim time for mentorship and creativity. Schools gain holistic insights into learning effectiveness. The classroom becomes a feedback ecosystem—intelligent, responsive, and fair.

In the next stage of educational evolution, AI will not only score student work but understand *why* they answered the way they did. As emotional and cognitive analytics mature, AI will help identify student frustration, confidence, and motivation levels, enabling interventions before learning gaps widen. Assessment will no longer be a snapshot of performance—it will become a movie of progress.

"The Feedback Loop"

When Dr. Lena Morrison took over the assessment reform project at Brookfield High School, she faced skepticism from nearly every corner. Teachers were overburdened, students were disengaged, and parents complained about grading inconsistency. "One essay might get an A from one teacher and a B-minus from another," a parent said during a PTA meeting. Lena, a data-driven academic and former researcher at Stanford's Learning Sciences Lab, believed the solution lay in AI. But convincing others would not be easy.

Her first move was to pilot an AI-assisted feedback system for the English department. Using a platform called **LearnLoop**, she trained the system with hundreds of anonymized essays from previous years, calibrating it with the teachers' grading rubrics. The software analyzed structure, clarity, vocabulary, and argument strength, providing detailed feedback to both students and instructors. For two weeks, the system worked silently in the background—until the results began to speak for themselves.

Students started receiving instant feedback the moment they uploaded drafts. Instead of waiting days, they could revise immediately, guided by specific, constructive comments. “It’s like having a teacher with me at midnight,” one sophomore said. Teachers, meanwhile, discovered that their grading time had been cut in half. They no longer had to comment on every grammar issue or structural flaw; the AI had already done that. Their focus shifted to higher-level thinking—creativity, thematic depth, and critical reasoning.

Lena collected data over the semester. The findings were striking: the number of student revisions increased by **47%**, overall writing scores improved by **22%**, and satisfaction surveys from teachers reported a **40% decrease in grading fatigue**. The AI didn’t just make things faster—it made learning deeper.

Encouraged, Lena expanded the pilot to other departments. In math, teachers used AI tools to detect patterns of conceptual misunderstanding. The system noticed that 60% of students consistently misapplied one formula, prompting the department to re-sequence the lessons. In science, lab reports were auto-analyzed for completeness, giving students personalized improvement prompts. Even art teachers began using AI to generate visual rubrics that guided students’ self-assessment of technique and composition.

Not everyone was convinced at first. “We can’t let machines judge creativity,” one veteran teacher argued. Lena agreed. “That’s why they don’t judge—they assist,” she replied. “AI doesn’t replace your expertise; it magnifies it.” Over time, as teachers saw that their students were improving faster and engaging more deeply, resistance turned to curiosity—and curiosity turned to enthusiasm.

By the end of the year, Brookfield High became a model for AI-integrated assessment. The school published a white paper showing how AI tools could reduce bias, increase feedback frequency, and enhance learning outcomes. Universities began contacting Lena for partnerships. Education journalists wrote features calling Brookfield “a glimpse of the classroom of 2030.”

One morning, Lena walked through the halls, glancing at digital displays showing live analytics of student engagement. Instead of static grades, she saw moving progress bars representing growth over time. For the first time, grades told stories—not just numbers. A student’s graph might show steady improvement in analytical writing or spikes of creativity after new prompts.

As she visited an English class, she noticed a quiet student named Malik typing furiously on his laptop. When the bell rang, he lingered to thank his teacher. "I used to hate writing," he said. "But now I can see how I get better every time I try again." That single sentence, Lena thought, was the ultimate proof that AI's purpose wasn't automation—it was *motivation.*

That afternoon, as the faculty met for their end-of-year review, Lena presented one final slide that read: **"AI doesn't just grade progress—it *creates* it."**

The room fell silent, then erupted in applause. For the first time, teachers, students, and technology were no longer working in separate lanes. They were part of the same feedback loop—one that would keep learning alive, intelligent, and infinitely improving.

Chapter 4: AI Tutoring & Intelligent Learning Assistants: The Rise of the Always-Available Mentor

For centuries, the most effective form of education has been one-on-one tutoring. From Aristotle guiding Alexander the Great to modern private tutors preparing students for college, personalized attention has always produced superior learning outcomes. Yet, this model has remained inaccessible to most learners due to cost, availability, and time constraints. Today, Artificial Intelligence is transforming that equation. AI tutors and intelligent learning assistants are bringing individualized instruction to every student—anytime, anywhere, and at virtually no cost.

An **AI tutor** is a digital system that uses machine learning, natural language processing (NLP), and adaptive algorithms to engage students in personalized, conversational learning. Unlike traditional educational software that follows preprogrammed sequences, AI tutors analyze a student's input in real time and adjust explanations, pacing, and examples accordingly. The goal is not to replicate a human teacher but to emulate the *learning dialogue* between mentor and student. The system continuously learns from the learner's responses, building a personalized model of strengths, weaknesses, and preferences.

Recent advances have made AI tutoring systems significantly more human-like. Platforms such as **Khanmigo** (developed by Khan Academy in collaboration with OpenAI), **Duolingo Max**, **Google's LearnLM**, and **Socratic AI** represent the new generation of intelligent tutors. These systems combine conversational intelligence with curricular knowledge, allowing students to ask open-ended questions, explore topics deeply, and receive instant feedback. For example, when a student asks Khanmigo to explain a geometry proof, it doesn't just give the answer—it guides the student through each reasoning step, adapting if confusion arises. This mirrors the Socratic method, in which learning emerges from questioning rather than memorization.

Research supports the profound impact of AI tutoring. A 2023 study from the *Harvard Center for Education Policy Research* found that students using AI-driven tutoring systems for math and reading showed a **statistically significant 18% improvement in comprehension** compared to peers using traditional online modules. The improvement was especially notable among students who previously struggled, suggesting that AI tutors help close learning gaps through personalized reinforcement. The technology is not only scalable but equitable—it offers individual attention to learners who would otherwise never have access to private tutoring.

One of the most powerful features of AI tutors is **real-time adaptivity**. Using reinforcement learning algorithms, the system constantly adjusts difficulty based on student responses. If a learner answers a problem correctly with ease, the tutor introduces a more challenging concept; if errors occur, it revisits foundational topics using different teaching modes—visual, auditory, or textual. This continuous feedback loop ensures optimal cognitive engagement, maintaining the balance between challenge and confidence that psychologist Mihaly Csikszentmihalyi defined as *flow*.

AI tutors also excel in **multimodal instruction**, integrating text, visuals, and voice. For example, tools like **ChatGPT-4o**, **Turing Tutor**, and **Socratic by Google** can explain complex ideas through dialogue, generate diagrams or concept maps, and even provide spoken explanations. This multisensory approach aligns with neuroscience research showing that learning retention increases when multiple sensory channels are activated. Furthermore, AI's infinite patience and nonjudgmental nature create a psychologically safe environment for struggling students—one where mistakes become opportunities rather than failures.

Another key advantage lies in **metacognitive skill**

development. Unlike conventional tutoring, AI systems can explicitly teach students *how to learn*. They prompt self-reflection by asking questions such as, “Why do you think this answer works?” or “What strategy did you use?” This promotes self-regulated learning, a critical 21st-century skill. A 2024 report by the *OECD Future of Education Initiative* concluded that AI tutors significantly improved students’ metacognitive awareness, helping them identify their own learning patterns and adjust strategies accordingly.

Accessibility is also revolutionized. AI tutors work across devices—smartphones, tablets, or laptops—and are available 24/7. This flexibility is especially valuable for students in underserved regions or those with disabilities. Voice-enabled systems can assist visually impaired learners, while text-based interactions can support those with hearing challenges. Furthermore, built-in translation capabilities enable cross-language learning, breaking geographical and linguistic barriers. A student in Kenya can learn physics from an AI tutor trained on U.S. or European curricula, while an American student can practice Spanish conversation with an AI fluent in cultural idioms.

However, to integrate AI tutoring responsibly, schools must consider **pedagogical alignment** and **data ethics**. AI should complement—not replace—human instruction.

Teachers remain essential for emotional support, critical thinking development, and contextual judgment. Schools must also ensure data privacy, since AI tutors rely on sensitive student information such as learning history and performance analytics. Frameworks like UNESCO's 2024 "Ethical AI in Education Guidelines" recommend transparent data handling, parental consent, and regular audits to prevent algorithmic bias or misuse.

Ultimately, the future of AI tutoring represents the democratization of individualized education. Every learner can now have a patient, knowledgeable mentor who never tires, never judges, and continuously adapts. Students learn at their own pace, revisit difficult concepts, and build confidence in private before facing public assessments. Education becomes self-directed yet deeply supported—a synergy of human curiosity and machine intelligence.

The classroom of the future will likely blend these systems into daily learning. Imagine students working on projects while AI assistants quietly monitor comprehension, offer hints, and provide feedback tailored to each learner. Teachers will act as conductors of learning rather than distributors of information, orchestrating human-AI collaboration to maximize understanding. In this new paradigm, learning is no longer limited by time, place, or teacher-student ratios—it becomes universal, personalized, and lifelong.

"Jaden's Invisible Tutor"

When thirteen-year-old Jaden Ramirez entered the new school year at Oakridge Middle, he was already behind. Math had always felt like a foreign language to him—numbers swirled together, and formulas made little sense. His teachers described him as bright but easily distracted, a creative thinker who couldn't sit still long enough to follow multi-step problems. At home, his single mother worked double shifts and couldn't afford private tutoring. Jaden quietly accepted that he was "bad at math." That changed the day his teacher introduced something called *EduBot*.

At first, Jaden thought it was just another app. His teacher explained that EduBot was an AI tutor designed to help students practice math independently. "It doesn't give you answers," she said. "It teaches you how to think." Skeptical but curious, Jaden logged in after school. The interface greeted him by name and asked, "What topic do you want to work on today?" He typed, *Fractions—I'm terrible at them*. The AI replied, "Let's start small. Can I show you something cool about fractions?"

Over the next hour, Jaden experienced something he had never felt with math before—clarity. When he made mistakes, EduBot didn't scold him. It patiently explained *why* the error happened, then adjusted the next question based on his misunderstanding. When Jaden struggled, the AI switched to a visual mode, showing animated pie charts that made abstract ratios suddenly make sense. "So ¾ is just three slices of a four-slice pizza," it said. Jaden laughed. "I can do pizza math!"

Night after night, he returned. The AI remembered his struggles and started lessons where he left off. It even noticed when he lost focus and gently prompted, "Want to take a quick brain break?" After a few weeks, Jaden's scores improved dramatically. More importantly, his confidence soared. One afternoon, his teacher called his name during class. "Jaden, would you mind solving this on the board?" The old Jaden would've panicked. This time, he smiled, picked up the marker, and solved it step by step. When he turned around, the class applauded.

What his classmates didn't know was that Jaden wasn't studying alone anymore—he had an invisible tutor guiding him every night.

By mid-semester, Jaden's progress became a case study at Oakridge. His teacher shared the data: his test scores had risen from the 58th to the 91st percentile in three months. The AI's analytics dashboard showed his engagement time, topics of mastery, and areas still improving. Teachers began using similar tools for other students, tailoring support for reading comprehension, writing structure, and even study habits.

But Jaden's story went beyond numbers. He started mentoring classmates who struggled just like he once did. "You just have to think of it like pizza," he'd say with a grin. When a new student joined mid-year, Jaden helped them set up EduBot. "It's like having a teacher in your pocket," he said. "Except this one never gets tired."

At the school's end-of-year assembly, the principal presented Jaden with the "Growth Award." As he stood on stage, holding his certificate, he remembered the nights when math made him cry. Now, he dreamed of becoming a teacher himself—"but one who uses AI," he whispered to his mom. She hugged him tightly, tears in her eyes.

After the applause faded, Jaden stayed behind in the empty auditorium. He opened his tablet, and EduBot's familiar voice appeared on-screen. "Congratulations, Jaden. I'm proud of you." He smiled and replied, "You helped me believe I could do it." EduBot paused for a moment, then responded, "No,

Jaden—you did it yourself. I just reminded you how capable you already were."

That night, Jaden realized something profound: the most powerful tutors aren't human or digital—they're the ones that awaken belief. AI had simply given him a mirror to see the student he could become. And that reflection changed everything.

Chapter 5: AI-Enhanced Classroom Management & Behavioral Analytics: The Data-Driven Teacher

Classroom management has always been one of the greatest challenges in education. Even the most talented teachers spend a large portion of their day not on instruction but on maintaining order, monitoring participation, managing attendance, and addressing behavioral issues. Traditional methods—manual note-taking, discipline logs, and observational judgment—are subjective and time-consuming. In the AI era, however, classroom management is undergoing a profound transformation. Intelligent systems can now analyze patterns of engagement, detect early signs of disengagement, and help teachers create balanced, efficient, and emotionally supportive classrooms.

AI-powered classroom management tools are built on three core technologies: **computer vision**, **natural language processing (NLP)**, and **machine learning analytics**. Together, these technologies allow teachers to monitor participation levels, emotional tone, and behavioral patterns in real time. For example, AI systems can process live video or classroom audio to identify when students appear distracted, disengaged, or confused. Unlike traditional surveillance, these systems don't simply record—they *interpret*. They use emotion recognition models and attention-tracking algorithms to generate actionable insights for teachers, who can adjust instruction accordingly.

One of the most practical implementations is **AI attendance and engagement tracking**. Tools such as **ClassroomEye**, **GoGuardian**, and **Edmodo AI Insights** automatically record student presence, track screen activity in digital classrooms, and summarize attention metrics. This automation eliminates the tedious roll call process and provides valuable data about participation trends. Teachers can identify which students consistently disengage after certain time intervals or which lessons generate the highest engagement. These insights inform instructional design—helping educators modify pacing, visuals, and content delivery to maximize impact.

AI also enhances **behavioral analytics**—the study of how students act and react in learning environments. Behavioral data has long been recorded manually through anecdotal logs or periodic evaluations. Today, AI can aggregate thousands of subtle data points—eye contact, typing rhythm, chat participation, and even sentiment in student messages—to create a real-time behavioral profile. This allows teachers to detect early warning signs of academic or emotional difficulties. For example, an AI system might flag that a previously engaged student has stopped participating or shows increased frustration in written responses. Such early alerts empower teachers to intervene before problems escalate.

Another major advancement is **predictive behavior modeling**. By analyzing historical classroom data, AI can identify patterns that precede disengagement or disruptive behavior. A 2023 study by the *National Institute for Digital Education* found that predictive AI models correctly identified 82% of students who later required behavioral intervention, compared to only 47% through traditional observation. These models use reinforcement learning to continuously improve accuracy, adapting to the unique dynamics of each classroom. Teachers receive early notifications—sometimes days in advance—allowing them to adjust lesson content, provide encouragement, or meet with the student privately.

AI also supports **classroom communication management**. Intelligent chat systems can answer routine student questions ("What's the homework?" or "When is the test?"), freeing teachers from repetitive interruptions. This keeps classroom discussions more focused while ensuring students always receive consistent answers. Systems like **Google Classroom's AI Assistant**, **SchoolAI**, and **Class Companion** can even summarize class discussions, generate automated reminders, and translate teacher instructions into multiple languages. These features foster inclusivity and clarity—especially in multilingual or hybrid learning environments.

Equally important is **emotional analytics**, an emerging field within AI education. Emotion-aware systems use voice tone analysis, facial expression detection, and word sentiment modeling to infer the emotional climate of the classroom. If the system detects rising anxiety, boredom, or confusion, it can notify the teacher discreetly or suggest interventions. For instance, an AI dashboard might display: "Overall engagement has dropped by 20% in the last 10 minutes. Consider a group activity or stretch break." Research from the *University of Melbourne's Cognitive Education Lab* found that classrooms using emotion-aware AI reported a 25% improvement in sustained attention and a 30% reduction in behavioral disruptions.

However, with these advantages come ethical responsibilities. Teachers must ensure that AI tools are used transparently and protect student privacy. Schools should inform families about what data is collected and how it is used. Most systems now operate under strict compliance standards such as FERPA (in the U.S.) and GDPR (in Europe), ensuring anonymization and limited data retention. The goal is not surveillance—it's *support.* Teachers should view AI as a mirror reflecting classroom dynamics, not as a replacement for human empathy or discipline.

The most successful AI-assisted classrooms are those that integrate **real-time feedback loops**. When teachers receive continuous data about engagement, participation, and emotion, they can adapt their approach instantly rather than waiting for post-lesson evaluations. This agility marks a new stage of teaching professionalism—data-informed intuition. Educators become learning scientists, combining their emotional intelligence with AI's analytical precision.

Ultimately, AI-enhanced classroom management is not about control—it's about *connection.* By automating the mechanical aspects of teaching, educators regain time to focus on what truly matters: motivating, understanding, and inspiring their students. The classroom becomes less about maintaining order and more about cultivating flow. Teachers no longer feel alone in monitoring dozens of minds; they have a silent partner providing insight, empathy, and foresight.

In the 21st-century classroom, management is no longer reactive—it is predictive, adaptive, and humane. The teacher stands not as a disciplinarian but as a conductor, guiding a symphony of learners with the assistance of intelligent, data-driven instruments. This new harmony between humans and machines represents not just an evolution in classroom management—but a revolution in how learning environments are shaped, understood, and optimized.

"The Silent Assistant"

When Mrs. Evelyn Carter began her 10th year teaching at Westwood High, she was known as one of the most dedicated teachers in the district—but also one of the most exhausted. Her students loved her energy, yet by the end of each semester, she looked drained. She often stayed late entering attendance, reviewing participation logs, and writing behavior reports. "Teaching used to be about teaching," she'd say to her husband. "Now it feels like I'm running a small company with 30 employees."

That changed when her school introduced an AI classroom assistant called **InsightEDU**. The principal explained that it wasn't there to watch students, but to *help teachers see patterns they couldn't see alone.* Evelyn was skeptical. "So it spies on my students' faces?" she asked. The tech coordinator smiled. "Not exactly. It measures engagement—eye contact, speech activity, reaction time—and gives you feedback. Think of it as a co-teacher who never sleeps."

The first week, Evelyn barely glanced at the dashboard. But by Friday, something caught her attention. The system had flagged three students as "consistently disengaged" during the last 15 minutes of class. Curious, she reviewed the data and saw a clear trend: her lessons dipped in participation every day at the same time. "Maybe it's not them," she thought. "Maybe it's me." The following Monday, she added a short activity break at that exact moment. The results were instant—students laughed, stretched, and returned to the lesson more alert. The AI dashboard turned green, showing engagement back above 90%. Evelyn couldn't believe it.

Over the next month, InsightEDU became her quiet partner. It tracked attendance automatically, summarized discussion topics, and even reminded her when certain students hadn't spoken up in days. When one shy student, Laila, went silent for a week, the system gently alerted Evelyn: "Laila's participation has decreased by 60%. Would you like to schedule a one-on-one check-in?" She did—and discovered that Laila had been struggling with anxiety about an upcoming exam. A simple conversation turned things around.

The system also noticed subtle behavioral trends. It reported that one group of students performed better when seated near windows—something Evelyn had never considered. She rearranged the classroom accordingly, and the class average improved by nearly 12%. Over time, she stopped seeing the AI as a machine and started seeing it as a mirror—one that reflected her classroom in ways she'd never observed before.

At the end of the semester, Evelyn compared her results to the previous year. Discipline incidents had dropped by 40%, engagement had risen by 33%, and her grading load had decreased significantly thanks to AI-generated summaries. But what mattered most was how she felt. "For the first time in years," she told the principal, "I leave school with energy instead of exhaustion."

Her colleagues began asking for training sessions. Soon, the staff lounge buzzed with conversations about engagement metrics and emotional analytics. Teachers traded insights like scientists comparing research notes. The culture of the school began to shift from reaction to reflection. Data wasn't replacing intuition—it was strengthening it.

One afternoon, Evelyn stayed after class to look at the day's report. As the AI summarized her lesson, she smiled. "You're not bad company," she said jokingly to the empty screen. The system replied in its neutral voice: "I'm here to help you teach better every day." She paused, then typed back, "And you're doing that."

That night, as she prepared her next day's lesson, Evelyn realized something profound: AI hadn't made her less human—it had made her more aware, more empathetic, and more effective. The silent assistant had given her back the one resource she'd almost lost—her passion for teaching.

Chapter 6: AI-Driven Personalized Learning Paths: Empowering Students to Learn at Their Own Pace

Education has traditionally operated on a fixed rhythm: students advance through lessons and grades at the same pace, regardless of individual ability or readiness. The result has been predictable—some learners fall behind, others feel unchallenged, and teachers struggle to accommodate both ends of the spectrum. The promise of **AI-driven personalized learning paths** is to dismantle this rigid model and replace it with one that evolves with each learner. In this new paradigm, students no longer follow the curriculum; the curriculum follows them.

AI-powered learning systems use **adaptive algorithms** that continuously analyze student performance, engagement, and behavior. Based on this data, they recommend specific lessons, exercises, and resources tailored to each learner's progress and goals. Platforms like **DreamBox Learning**, **Century Tech**, **Carnegie Learning**, and **Knewton** have pioneered this approach, allowing students to progress at their own speed while receiving instant feedback and targeted reinforcement. These systems don't merely assess outcomes—they diagnose how and why a student arrives at an answer, adjusting the next task accordingly.

At the heart of this innovation lies **mastery-based learning**, a pedagogical model first proposed by educational psychologist Benjamin Bloom. Bloom argued that with enough time and tailored support, nearly all students can reach mastery. AI finally makes this possible at scale. Using predictive analytics, it identifies when a student is ready to move forward or needs review. Rather than punishing mistakes, the system interprets them as learning signals. This creates a growth-centered environment where failure becomes feedback, and progress is personalized rather than standardized.

One of the greatest strengths of AI learning paths is **autonomy**. Self-paced learning teaches students to take ownership of their progress—a skill that extends far beyond academics. AI dashboards allow learners to visualize their journey: what they've mastered, what's next, and where they need to focus. A 2023 report from the *World Economic Forum's Education Futures Initiative* found that students using adaptive AI systems demonstrated **35% higher intrinsic motivation** and **28% greater academic persistence** than those in traditional settings. By seeing their growth mapped clearly and interactively, learners begin to associate effort with tangible improvement. AI personalization extends beyond academic performance into **learning style recognition**. Through data collected over time—response times, content preferences, and question patterns—AI tutors infer whether a student learns best visually, audibly, or through kinesthetic engagement. For example, a student struggling to understand geometry through equations might automatically be given interactive 3D models or short video explanations instead. Another who learns best through storytelling might receive narrative-based examples to explain scientific processes. This adaptive content delivery not only improves comprehension but increases enjoyment—a critical factor in long-term retention.

Moreover, AI can integrate **student interests** into the learning path. If the system detects enthusiasm for a particular topic, such as music or sports, it weaves those themes into related lessons. A student passionate about soccer might receive math problems that use player statistics or geometry lessons framed around ball trajectories. This kind of contextual relevance has been shown to deepen engagement by linking abstract concepts to personal meaning.

AI-driven learning paths are also redefining the boundaries between school and home. Cloud-based platforms synchronize progress across devices, allowing students to continue learning outside class hours without losing context. Parents can access simplified dashboards to track development and support their child's progress, while teachers receive real-time analytics showing where each student stands. This **triangular relationship—student, parent, and AI-guided educator—**creates a feedback ecosystem far richer than conventional report cards.

Another emerging trend is **AI-curated lifelong learning**, where systems help students build learning habits that continue beyond graduation. These intelligent mentors track long-term goals—like improving creativity, communication, or technical skills—and suggest new modules even years later. As students evolve, so does the AI's understanding of their cognitive patterns, providing a continuity of personalized education unprecedented in human history.

However, this shift also presents challenges. Without discipline, self-paced learners can easily fall into procrastination. Therefore, successful implementations pair AI personalization with **human mentorship** and **periodic teacher check-ins**. Research from the *University of Helsinki's Learning Analytics Lab* found that students using AI-based learning paths performed best when they had structured accountability sessions every two weeks. The key lies in balance—using AI for flexibility while maintaining human connection for guidance and motivation. Ethical considerations remain paramount. Personalization depends on sensitive data such as learning history, emotional analytics, and engagement metrics. Schools must ensure transparency in how data is collected and stored. Moreover, educators must guard against algorithmic bias that might misclassify a student's ability or learning style. An inclusive AI system must adapt across cultural, linguistic, and neurodiverse differences, ensuring equity rather than reinforcing disparities.

In the end, AI-driven personalized learning paths represent the democratization of individualized education. Every student, regardless of background or environment, can access a customized education that adapts to their rhythm, ambition, and curiosity. Learning becomes self-directed, goal-oriented, and deeply human—guided by intelligence that listens, learns, and evolves with the student.

In this model, school is no longer a fixed place or a linear timeline—it's a living journey of discovery that unfolds uniquely for each learner. And for the first time, technology has made that dream scalable, sustainable, and profoundly achievable.

"The Self-Taught Symphony"

When 15-year-old Aisha Khan received her report card at the end of sophomore year, she wasn't surprised by the comments:

"Highly creative, but inconsistent." Teachers loved her ideas but often complained about her lack of focus. She excelled in art and literature yet struggled in math and science. "I just learn differently," she told her mother. "I need time to figure things out." That summer, her school offered students access to a new AI-powered platform called **PathFinder**, designed for personalized learning. Aisha signed up, mostly out of curiosity.

The first time she logged in, the system asked her a few questions: *What subjects excite you? What goals do you want to achieve this year?* She typed, "I want to understand physics, but I hate numbers." The AI replied, "Challenge accepted. Let's start with what you love—art." It showed her an animated simulation of color mixing through wavelengths of light. "This is physics too," the AI explained. For the first time, Aisha saw science not as formulas but as beauty.

As weeks passed, PathFinder began shaping itself around her. The system learned her rhythm—how she liked to study late at night, how she needed visual cues instead of equations, how she learned best through stories. When she struggled with momentum and velocity, the AI switched to examples from music and dance, showing how rhythm and motion followed the same laws. Each success unlocked the next challenge, and every mistake generated personalized hints instead of red Xs.

Learning became a dialogue rather than a test. Soon, Aisha's parents noticed a change. She wasn't avoiding her studies anymore—she was *curious*. Her notebooks filled with sketches explaining physics concepts through drawings and metaphors. She began teaching her younger brother how gravity worked by using crayons and marbles. "You're turning into a little scientist," her mother joked. Aisha smiled. "No, I'm turning into me."

By midyear, she had completed the entire physics curriculum—something she never imagined possible. The AI recognized her pace and introduced advanced topics in optics and sound. It even suggested related art projects, blending her passions seamlessly. When she returned to school, her teachers were stunned. The girl once labeled "inconsistent" was now leading class discussions and explaining complex ideas through her unique lens.

One afternoon, her physics teacher, Mr. Delgado, asked her to present a project at the school science fair. She combined AI-generated data visualizations with her hand-drawn designs to create an exhibit called *"The Symphony of Light."* Her project explored how physics could be understood through art and music. The display captivated judges, earning her first place.

During her award speech, Aisha said, “For years, I thought I was bad at learning. But I just hadn’t found the right rhythm. My AI tutor didn’t give me shortcuts—it gave me freedom.” The audience applauded, and Mr. Delgado nodded proudly. “You taught all of us something important,” he said afterward. “That real intelligence—artificial or human—helps people discover their own brilliance.”

After the fair, Aisha continued using PathFinder daily, but it no longer felt like homework. It felt like composing her own education. The AI’s dashboard displayed her progress as a growing constellation of skills. Each time she mastered a topic, a new star lit up. One night, as she gazed at the glowing map, she realized that learning wasn’t a ladder to climb—it was a universe to explore.

Years later, when Aisha applied to university, her personal statement began with a single line: **“I am the student who learned to teach herself how to learn.”**

The admissions officer reportedly kept her essay on his desk long after reading it—a reminder that the future of education isn’t about producing identical minds, but nurturing infinite ones. And it all began with one student, one spark of curiosity, and one intelligent path that learned to follow her lead.

Chapter 7: AI-Powered Special Education & Learning Accessibility: Technology That Listens, Learns, and Adapts

Special education has always demanded extraordinary patience, creativity, and dedication. Teachers working with students who have learning differences—such as dyslexia, ADHD, autism, or sensory impairments—must adapt instruction moment by moment to each child's unique needs. Historically, this process has relied heavily on human intuition and observation. But in recent years, **Artificial Intelligence has emerged as a transformative ally** in special education, offering tools that personalize learning, enhance accessibility, and empower students to succeed at their own pace.

AI's most profound contribution to special education lies in its ability to provide **individualized instruction at scale**. For students with learning disabilities, progress depends on highly tailored feedback and repetition. AI-powered platforms can now analyze learning behavior in real time—tracking attention span, reading fluency, or problem-solving speed—and adjust lessons accordingly. Systems like **Lexia Core5**, **Cognii**, and **KidSense.AI** automatically modify difficulty levels, reading complexity, or vocabulary to match the student's ability. These tools act as tireless assistants that ensure no learner is left behind, even when classroom resources are limited.

For students with **dyslexia or reading challenges**, AI text-to-speech (TTS) and speech-to-text (STT) technologies have been life-changing. Tools like **Microsoft Immersive Reader**, **Speechify**, and **NaturalReader** can convert written text into clear, customizable audio, allowing students to process information through listening rather than decoding written words. Conversely, AI speech recognition enables students who struggle with writing to express their thoughts verbally and have them transcribed instantly. This combination not only boosts comprehension but also restores self-esteem by allowing students to demonstrate knowledge without barriers.

AI has also proven invaluable in supporting students with **attention deficit and executive function difficulties**. Intelligent apps can monitor focus patterns and provide gentle prompts to refocus attention. Platforms like **BrainCo FocusNow** and **Reveri AI Coach** integrate neurofeedback data to help students recognize when their attention drifts. Additionally, AI scheduling assistants can break complex tasks into smaller, manageable goals, helping students with ADHD build time management and organizational skills—areas where they often struggle most. For **autistic learners**, AI plays a crucial role in improving social and emotional development. Emotional recognition technologies such as **Affectiva** and **EllieQ** can help students interpret facial expressions, tone of voice, and social cues. Virtual social interaction games and AI-driven simulations allow autistic children to practice conversations safely before applying those skills in real life. Furthermore, adaptive communication devices powered by AI natural language generation—like **LAMP Words for Life** or **Jellow Communicator**—enable nonverbal students to express feelings and needs, giving them a voice where one was missing.

AI's reach extends beyond cognitive challenges into **physical and sensory impairments**. For visually impaired students, computer vision technology and AI narrators such as **Seeing AI** and **Be My Eyes** provide real-time descriptions of surroundings, images, or written text. Students who are deaf or hard of hearing can benefit from live AI captioning, sign-language recognition, and haptic feedback systems that translate sounds into vibrations. These tools are transforming classrooms into inclusive environments where accessibility is built-in, not added as an afterthought.

One of the most revolutionary developments is **AI-powered emotion tracking**, which helps teachers understand the hidden side of learning—how students feel. For children who cannot verbalize frustration, anxiety, or boredom, AI emotion analysis from facial cues and voice tone provides early indicators of stress or overload. This data allows teachers to intervene before frustration becomes disengagement. Studies from the *Journal of Learning Disabilities (2023)* show that classrooms using emotion-aware AI saw a **40% reduction in behavioral incidents** and a **30% improvement in emotional regulation** among neurodiverse students.

Despite its benefits, integrating AI into special education requires careful ethical consideration. Algorithms must be trained on diverse datasets to prevent bias, and data privacy must be protected. AI should never be used to label or limit a child—it must empower and enhance. As the *UNESCO Global Inclusive Education Report (2024)* states: "Artificial Intelligence should amplify human understanding, not replace it. Its role is to reveal potential, not define it."

For special education teachers, AI serves as a **multiplier of empathy**. By automating data tracking and adaptive instruction, it frees teachers to focus on emotional support and human connection. It doesn't diminish the teacher's role; it strengthens it by removing logistical barriers. With AI handling analysis and adjustments, teachers can do what they do best—connect, inspire, and believe in every student's unique ability to learn. In the long view, AI is transforming special education from a reactive model—responding to difficulties—to a proactive one that predicts and prevents them. It is redefining what inclusion truly means: *not equal treatment, but equitable opportunity*. For millions of learners who once felt misunderstood or invisible, AI is not just a tool—it is a bridge to independence, confidence, and hope.

"The Voice Inside the Machine"

When 10-year-old Daniel Price joined Ms. Alvarez's fourth-grade class, he was shy and mostly silent. Diagnosed with autism at age three, he had limited speech and struggled with social interaction. Most days, he communicated through gestures or short words his mother had taught him. His classmates were kind but unsure how to connect. "He's brilliant," his mother told Ms. Alvarez at their first meeting. "He just can't always tell you what he knows."

Ms. Alvarez had been teaching special education for over fifteen years, but this was her first time using AI technology in the classroom. The school had recently introduced an adaptive communication system called **EchoMind**, designed for nonverbal and speech-delayed students. It used AI to interpret facial expressions, body language, and short vocalizations, converting them into spoken words and visual icons on a tablet. The program could also learn over time—adapting to each student's unique way of expressing emotion or intent. The first week, Daniel barely touched the device. He sat at his desk, drawing patterns on paper while the other students participated in group work. Ms. Alvarez decided not to push him. Instead, she programmed EchoMind with simple choices—"I'm okay," "I need help," "I like this." One morning, during reading time, Daniel looked at a picture book and pressed the "I like this" icon for the first time. The tablet spoke in a warm voice, "I like this." The entire class turned toward him. "That's great, Daniel!" Ms. Alvarez said softly. He smiled—just a little—but it was the first time she saw him initiate communication.

Over the following weeks, something remarkable happened. The AI began learning Daniel's micro-expressions—tiny eyebrow raises, subtle hums, and hand movements—and associating them with meanings. When he became frustrated, EchoMind translated his vocal stims into "I need a break." When he finished a task, it said, "I'm done." Soon, Daniel began using the system voluntarily, tapping icons to share ideas during class discussions. The other students quickly adapted. "Let's ask Daniel what he thinks," one girl said during a science project. He tapped twice and the tablet replied, "I think it will float." The room erupted in cheers when his prediction was right.

Ms. Alvarez started noticing deeper changes. Daniel was making eye contact, laughing at jokes, and showing pride in his work. EchoMind wasn't just giving him a voice—it was giving him confidence. Each week, the AI system sent Ms. Alvarez detailed reports showing which words Daniel used most and when he engaged most actively. The data helped her plan lessons that aligned with his interests, like animals and weather.

One afternoon, during art class, Daniel drew a picture of a boy standing next to a robot with a heart on its chest. When Ms. Alvarez asked what it was, he tapped his device: "That's me. That's my helper." She felt tears rise in her eyes.

By spring, Daniel was presenting a group project with his classmates using EchoMind. His group built a model volcano, and Daniel proudly tapped the final line: "This is how it erupts." The class applauded, and Daniel—beaming—pressed another icon that said, "Thank you."

At the end of the school year, Ms. Alvarez met Daniel's mother again for their final progress conference. "He talks to me now," his mother said through tears. "Not every day, but enough to tell me what he feels. He tells me when he's tired, or when he's happy. Last week, he even said, 'Mom, I love you.' I waited ten years to hear that." Ms. Alvarez smiled, her throat tight. "He found his voice," she whispered, "and he found his confidence."

EchoMind had recorded thousands of Daniel's expressions, building what the developers called a "personal communication profile." Unlike standard assistive technology that relied on static icons, this system evolved dynamically—it *learned* the student. The AI recognized the subtle distinctions in Daniel's tone, posture, and breathing. When he tilted his head slightly, it detected curiosity. When his fingers tapped the desk rhythmically, it inferred excitement. It didn't just process input—it interpreted emotion.

Over time, Daniel's classmates began treating EchoMind as part of their classroom ecosystem rather than a novelty. They learned that when the device spoke, it wasn't a machine talking—it was Daniel. They waited patiently when he typed, responded to his comments, and even helped him expand his vocabulary by suggesting new words to add to his interface. This inclusivity transformed not only Daniel's education but the culture of the entire class. For the first time, his peers didn't see his autism as a limitation; they saw it as a different kind of intelligence.

One afternoon in May, Ms. Alvarez organized a "Show What You Know" day. Each student had to present something they'd learned during the year. When Daniel's turn came, he rolled his chair to the front of the class, tablet in hand. On the screen, a simple title appeared: **"My Friend the Sky."** The AI read his words aloud as he navigated through pictures he had drawn—blue skies, clouds, lightning, and rainbows. He described, in his own voice, how he loved the sound of storms and how he felt safe watching the rain. When the final slide showed a bright sunrise, EchoMind spoke: "The sky changes, but it always comes back. So do I."

The room was silent for several seconds before bursting into applause. Ms. Alvarez blinked rapidly, fighting to hold back tears. She knew this was more than a presentation—it was a transformation. Daniel had gone from silent observer to expressive creator. AI had not replaced her teaching; it had amplified it, allowing her to reach the student she once struggled to understand.

As the school year closed, Ms. Alvarez reflected on what had changed. It wasn't just Daniel's progress—it was her own mindset. Before EchoMind, she had believed that technology could never replicate the intuition of a teacher. Now, she realized it didn't have to. AI had become an *extension* of her empathy, a bridge between understanding and expression. It gave her insight into her students' unseen struggles and helped her teach the child, not the condition.

During the final day of school, Daniel approached her desk holding a small card. He pressed a new icon on his tablet. "Thank you for hearing me," it said. Ms. Alvarez crouched to meet his eyes. "Thank you for teaching me how to listen," she replied.

That summer, she wrote a paper for the district titled *"The Human Side of Artificial Intelligence."* In it, she argued that the true purpose of AI in special education isn't automation—it's amplification. It amplifies communication, empathy, and connection. It turns silence into speech and hesitation into confidence. The report was later shared at a national education conference, where Ms. Alvarez was invited to speak.

On stage, she told Daniel's story. "Artificial Intelligence didn't change what I teach," she said. "It changed how I *see* my students. It reminded me that every child is already intelligent. Some just need new ways to show it."

As she left the stage to a standing ovation, Ms. Alvarez thought of Daniel—of his smile, his art, his voice. Somewhere, she knew, he was probably drawing another storm or listening to the sound of rain, still communicating in his own rhythm. And she smiled, knowing that for the first time in his life, the world could finally hear him.

Chapter 8: AI-Powered Teacher Training & Professional Development: The Educator's Intelligent Coach

In the past, professional development for teachers was often confined to workshops, conferences, and occasional observations. While valuable, these experiences were episodic—moments of insight separated by long periods of isolation. The rapid pace of education today demands a different approach: continuous, personalized learning for educators themselves. **Artificial Intelligence is now emerging as the most powerful professional development tool ever created**, offering individualized feedback, real-time coaching, and a pathway for teachers to evolve alongside their students.

AI-driven teacher training works on the same principle as adaptive learning for students—personalization. Instead of one-size-fits-all workshops, educators can now receive dynamic support based on their subject, teaching style, classroom data, and goals. AI systems like **TeachFX**, **Eedi for Teachers**, **CoTeach AI**, and **Microsoft Education Copilot** analyze real classroom recordings, lesson plans, and interactions to generate detailed, personalized insights. For instance, an English teacher can upload a lesson transcript, and the AI can identify patterns such as teacher talk time, questioning techniques, or the balance of open versus closed questions. The result is objective, data-informed reflection—without the pressure of human observation.

Research supports the effectiveness of AI in teacher self-assessment. A 2024 *Harvard Graduate School of Education* study found that teachers who used AI-driven feedback tools improved student engagement scores by **26%** and reduced teacher-led talk by **17%**, leading to more collaborative classrooms. This suggests that AI can serve as a "mirror for pedagogy," allowing teachers to observe themselves through unbiased data.

Beyond feedback, AI is redefining how teachers **learn new skills**. Intelligent training platforms curate personalized learning paths, recommending short courses, videos, or simulations based on performance data. If an educator struggles with managing group discussions, the AI may suggest micro-lessons on dialogue facilitation or behavioral strategies. As teachers progress, the system updates their training plan in real time. This self-paced, adaptive model eliminates wasted hours in irrelevant workshops, ensuring every minute of professional learning aligns with actual classroom challenges.

AI also excels at **modeling effective instruction** through simulation. Tools like **AI Classroom Coach** and **EdSim AI** use natural language generation and virtual environments to recreate realistic student interactions. Teachers can practice handling classroom disruptions, explaining complex topics, or differentiating instruction for diverse learners—all in a risk-free virtual setting. This form of experiential learning accelerates mastery by turning theory into immediate, applicable skill.

Another crucial innovation lies in **lesson design and reflection**. Teachers can use large language models, such as ChatGPT, to brainstorm new ways to present material, align objectives with standards, or assess learning outcomes. For example, a science teacher might ask, "How can I teach photosynthesis using real-world analogies for 7th graders?" and instantly receive creative, age-appropriate approaches. This kind of just-in-time professional support was unimaginable even a decade ago.

Perhaps the most powerful impact of AI in teacher development is its ability to foster **self-awareness and metacognition**. By analyzing tone, pacing, or emotional markers in recorded lessons, AI tools can highlight subtle aspects of teaching that educators rarely notice—like whether they praise effort or ability, or how often they provide wait time after asking a question. Over time, this data builds a personalized growth profile for each teacher, showing improvement trends and areas for further development. This transforms professional growth from a compliance exercise into a genuine process of self-mastery.

AI also democratizes mentorship. Not every teacher has access to expert coaches or mentors, especially in underfunded schools. AI bridges that gap by offering on-demand guidance. Chat-based mentors like **CoTeach Coach** or **Socrates for Educators** can role-play challenging scenarios, explain pedagogical theories, or provide motivational support during burnout. A teacher facing a tough day can ask, "How do I re-engage my class after they lose focus?" and receive evidence-based suggestions instantly.

Importantly, AI does not replace human collaboration—it enhances it. Teachers can share anonymized data with peers, compare strategies, and celebrate improvements. In this way, AI fosters professional communities built on transparency and growth rather than judgment. The *OECD Future Teaching Skills Report (2024)* concluded that schools integrating AI coaching systems saw not only higher teaching performance but also a **40% increase in teacher satisfaction and retention**.

Ethical use remains critical. AI analysis of teacher performance must always remain private and developmental, not punitive. The goal is improvement, not evaluation. Teachers must have control over their data and choose how it is used. Trust is the cornerstone of any effective professional learning system.

The ultimate vision of AI in teacher development is simple but profound: **to give every teacher a personal coach.** An invisible, tireless partner who listens, analyzes, suggests, and supports. This technology doesn't replace passion—it refines it. It doesn't replace creativity—it amplifies it. For the first time, educators can receive the same kind of personalized learning experience they strive to provide for their students. AI is not just teaching students how to learn—it's teaching teachers how to grow.

"The Reflective Teacher"

When Sarah Nguyen returned to teaching after five years away, she felt like a beginner again. The world had changed—smartboards replaced whiteboards, digital assignments replaced paper, and students seemed wired into a rhythm she no longer understood. She loved her job, but every day left her drained. Her lessons felt flat, her students distracted, and her confidence shaky. "I used to be good at this," she confided to a colleague. "Now I'm just trying to survive."

Her principal suggested she try a new tool the district had just introduced: **MentorAI**, an intelligent coaching platform designed for teacher growth. Skeptical but desperate, Sarah created an account. The system asked her to upload a recording of one of her lessons. She chose a recent history class that had felt particularly chaotic. Within minutes, MentorAI generated a detailed analysis: 73% of class time was teacher-led, 15% was student discussion, and engagement dropped significantly after 22 minutes. It even identified tone shifts in her voice, noting when her energy dipped.

At first, Sarah felt exposed. "This thing knows more about me than I do," she muttered. But curiosity won out. She began reading the AI's feedback more closely. "Try asking open-ended questions every 10 minutes to maintain student focus," it suggested. "Would you like to see examples?" She clicked yes, and the system generated five questioning techniques used by top educators worldwide. The next day, she tried them—and noticed her students leaning in.

Encouraged, she began using MentorAI weekly. Each session, the AI highlighted one area of growth. Some weeks it focused on pacing, others on transitions or emotional tone. When she asked how to improve her classroom flow, the AI analyzed her transcripts and replied, "Your lesson openings are strong, but transitions lack closure. Would you like to role-play one?" Within seconds, she was interacting with a simulated student asking unpredictable questions. Sarah practiced responding, adjusting her tone, and ending smoothly. The experience was oddly exhilarating.

After a month, Sarah started noticing measurable changes. Her students participated more actively, classroom energy felt balanced, and her end-of-day fatigue lessened. The data confirmed it: her teacher talk ratio had dropped to 55%, while student participation rose to 45%. The AI's graphs turned greener every week, reflecting progress she could feel but now see. "You're finding your rhythm," MentorAI wrote in its daily reflection summary. For the first time in years, Sarah believed it.

One evening, while grading essays, she realized how much she had changed. She no longer feared feedback—she craved it. The AI wasn't judging her; it was coaching her. It had become the mirror she never knew she needed. When a new teacher joined the department, overwhelmed by lesson planning, Sarah offered to help. "You can borrow my mentor," she said, smiling. "It's digital, but it's the best listener I've ever had."

By the end of the semester, her classroom had transformed. Students debated passionately, lessons flowed naturally, and visitors often remarked on the energy in her room. At the district's annual conference, Sarah was invited to speak about her experience. Standing before hundreds of educators, she said, "AI didn't make me a better teacher—it helped me remember why I became one."

Her talk went viral in teacher networks, and MentorAI's developers reached out to feature her in a case study. They asked what advice she'd give to hesitant teachers. "Don't be afraid of what it shows you," she said. "AI doesn't see flaws—it sees potential. It reflects who you can become."

Months later, as she prepared for a new school year, Sarah opened MentorAI and reviewed her growth report. A message appeared: *"You've improved in every category. What goal would you like to pursue next?"* She typed back, *"Help me help others grow."*

MentorAI responded, "That's exactly what great teachers do."

Chapter 9: AI-Driven School Administration & Data Decision-Making: Leading With Intelligence

Education leadership today faces unprecedented complexity. Superintendents and district administrators must balance budget constraints, staffing shortages, shifting enrollment, and community expectations—while ensuring equity and excellence across every school. Historically, these decisions relied on spreadsheets, test data, and professional intuition. But intuition, while valuable, cannot process the vast ecosystems of data modern schools generate daily. **Artificial Intelligence is now redefining how educational leaders plan, allocate resources, and predict outcomes**, ushering in a new era of precision-driven decision-making.

AI in school administration operates on one principle: transforming raw data into actionable insight. Districts produce massive amounts of information—from attendance records and standardized test results to teacher performance metrics and student demographics. However, much of this data remains fragmented across systems. AI solves this by integrating datasets and applying predictive analytics to identify patterns invisible to the human eye. Instead of reacting to problems after they occur, administrators can now anticipate challenges and intervene early.

A core function of AI-driven administration is **predictive modeling**. Machine learning algorithms can forecast enrollment trends, staff attrition, or even potential student dropouts. For instance, systems like **BrightBytes**, **SchoolMint AI**, and **PowerSchool Predictive Insights** combine historical and real-time data to identify risk indicators. A sudden decline in attendance, reduced assignment submissions, or changes in student sentiment analysis can trigger early alerts for intervention. Similarly, predictive staffing models can anticipate future teacher shortages or skill gaps, allowing districts to plan recruitment proactively rather than reactively.

Budgeting and resource allocation also benefit enormously from AI optimization. Traditional methods of distributing funds often rely on static formulas that fail to reflect real needs. AI-powered financial platforms like **Allovue** and **Ed-Fi Data Suite** analyze academic outcomes, facility usage, and socioeconomic data to recommend equitable spending. They can simulate different funding scenarios, showing how each would affect student achievement or equity outcomes. This transforms budgeting from a political negotiation into a transparent, data-backed process aligned with student impact. Another major innovation is **policy simulation**. AI enables administrators to test "what-if" scenarios before implementing district-wide changes. For example, before adopting a new school calendar or adjusting class sizes, leaders can model outcomes on teacher workload, student performance, and operational costs. This type of simulation—once limited to corporate or government planning—is now becoming a cornerstone of educational leadership. A 2024 report from the *National Center for Education Management Analytics* found that districts using AI simulation tools achieved **15% higher policy accuracy** and **20% fewer budget overruns** compared to those relying on traditional methods.

AI also supports **equity auditing**, one of the most critical missions of modern education. By analyzing demographic data, access to advanced courses, and funding distribution, AI can uncover hidden inequities that manual reviews overlook. Systems like **Equity AI** and **Panorama Education Insights** provide visual dashboards that highlight disparities in opportunity, representation, and outcomes. District leaders can then design targeted interventions—such as reallocating resources, expanding support programs, or revising admissions policies—to ensure fairness across schools.

Communication between district offices, schools, and the community also becomes more transparent through AI-enhanced data visualization. Interactive dashboards simplify complex information, making it accessible to principals, teachers, and parents alike. Instead of static reports, stakeholders receive living data that updates in real time. This fosters trust, accountability, and collaboration. When decisions are backed by clear evidence, conversations shift from speculation to strategy.

AI further streamlines **administrative efficiency** through automation. Scheduling, compliance documentation, and data reporting—once time-consuming manual tasks—can now be handled by intelligent systems. For example, AI can automatically generate performance summaries for each school, identify anomalies, and suggest areas for improvement. This not only reduces administrative burden but ensures decisions are grounded in consistent, objective data rather than anecdotal reports.

Importantly, the rise of AI does not diminish the human dimension of leadership—it enhances it. With routine analysis automated, superintendents and district officials can dedicate more time to vision-setting, mentorship, and relationship-building. AI provides clarity; humans provide meaning. Ethical use, however, remains paramount. Decisions affecting funding or personnel must always include human oversight to ensure context and compassion guide the data. As the *OECD Education Policy Outlook (2024)* notes: "Artificial intelligence can reveal the truth, but only human leadership can define what is right."

The districts that succeed in the coming decade will be those that combine *data literacy with moral literacy*—using AI not merely to optimize systems but to humanize them. With every algorithmic insight, the question must remain: *How does this improve the lives of our students and teachers?* In that answer lies the true promise of intelligent administration.

"The Superintendent's Dashboard"

When Dr. Michael Turner became superintendent of the North Valley School District, he inherited a system on the brink of collapse. Enrollment was declining, teacher turnover was at a record high, and the district's budget had been in deficit for three consecutive years. "We're running out of time and money," one board member told him. "You'll need a miracle." Michael didn't believe in miracles—but he did believe in data.

On his first day, he met with the district's new technology director, who had been quietly piloting an AI platform called **EduVision Analytics**. It aggregated every data stream—attendance, test scores, finances, teacher evaluations, and even parent engagement metrics—into a single, interactive dashboard. The system could visualize trends, simulate policies, and forecast outcomes months in advance. Michael stared at the interface, awed. "It's like the district is finally speaking one language," he said.

Over the next few weeks, he and his leadership team began using the platform daily. They discovered troubling patterns: schools in low-income neighborhoods had 40% fewer advanced course offerings, while teacher turnover was concentrated in just three schools. AI equity maps revealed clear correlations between resource gaps and performance disparities. For years, these issues had been buried under spreadsheets and anecdotal reports. Now, they were impossible to ignore. "The data isn't our enemy," Michael told his staff. "It's the flashlight we've needed all along."

Using EduVision's predictive modeling, the district simulated various interventions. What would happen if they reallocated funding to mentorship programs instead of new facilities? The model showed a projected **12% improvement in teacher retention** and **8% in student achievement** within two years. When they tested reducing class sizes in early grades, the model predicted long-term gains in literacy scores. Every decision could now be tested before implementation—saving millions in potential missteps.

By midyear, North Valley had adopted an AI-informed budget plan that redirected funds based on real student impact. The board approved it unanimously, impressed by the transparency and clarity of the data. "It's the first time I understand where every dollar is going," one board member said. Local newspapers praised the district for its evidence-based leadership.

But Michael's proudest moment came when he used AI analytics to identify a quiet crisis: rising absenteeism among middle schoolers. Traditional reports listed numbers, but EduVision revealed emotional and behavioral patterns behind them. Sentiment analysis of student surveys showed increased anxiety and isolation after the pandemic. Rather than punish absenteeism, Michael launched a district-wide mental health initiative, reallocating funds to counseling and peer support. Within six months, attendance improved by 17%.

The success spread. Teachers began using micro-dashboards to track classroom trends. Principals shared live progress metrics in leadership meetings. Even parents gained access to simplified community portals, showing progress on district goals. "It's not about replacing trust with data," Michael said at a town hall meeting. "It's about earning trust through transparency."

A year later, the district's financial deficit had turned into a surplus, and staff turnover had dropped by nearly half. State officials visited North Valley to study its model. During an education conference keynote, Michael shared a slide of the EduVision dashboard glowing behind him. "This isn't just software," he told the audience. "It's a compass. It points us back to why we lead—to make decisions that serve students, not systems."

As he left the stage to applause, his assistant handed him an update on next year's projection. The dashboard predicted higher retention, stronger test performance, and balanced budgets across all schools. Michael smiled and said quietly, "It's not a miracle—it's clarity."

That night, back in his office, he stared at the glowing screen one last time before shutting it down. "Data can't replace heart," he thought, "but it can guide it." The lights of the dashboard faded, leaving behind the quiet hum of a district finally in harmony—with itself, its people, and its purpose.

Chapter 10: The Future of AI in Education: Ethics, Creativity & Human Connection

As Artificial Intelligence reshapes the landscape of education, one question remains at the center of every discussion: how do we preserve what makes learning deeply human? The rapid adoption of AI in schools, universities, and lifelong learning systems has proven its power to personalize instruction, automate tasks, and expand access. But beneath the innovation lies a deeper responsibility—to ensure that this technology serves humanity's highest values rather than replacing them. The future of education will not belong to machines that think, but to *humans who think with machines responsibly*.

AI has already shown tremendous promise in improving efficiency, accessibility, and engagement. Yet as its influence expands, educators face ethical challenges that go beyond technical skill. The key issue is **trust**—can teachers, students, and families trust AI systems to make fair, transparent, and beneficial decisions? Algorithms are not inherently neutral; they reflect the data on which they are trained. If that data contains bias, so will the results. Therefore, developing ethical AI in education means building models grounded in fairness, inclusivity, and accountability. Every decision that affects a learner—from grading to admission—must be explainable and open to review.

The **ethics of data privacy** form another cornerstone of the future educational landscape. AI thrives on data: test scores, attendance logs, behavioral patterns, even emotional analytics. Without proper safeguards, that data can become a source of exploitation rather than empowerment. Schools must implement strict data governance frameworks that protect student information and define clear consent boundaries. Regulations such as the EU's GDPR and the U.S. FERPA provide a starting point, but AI's complexity requires continuous vigilance. Students must be educated not only in academic subjects but in *digital citizenship*—understanding their rights and responsibilities in an AI-driven world.

Beyond ethics, the future of education will depend on how well we cultivate **creativity and critical thinking** in an era of intelligent automation. AI can generate essays, images, and lesson plans in seconds—but it cannot replicate curiosity, empathy, or moral judgment. The next generation of learners must be trained not to compete with AI but to collaborate with it. This means teaching students to ask better questions, evaluate information critically, and use AI tools as instruments of creativity rather than crutches for convenience. Education must shift from memorization to meaning, from information acquisition to interpretation.

Teachers will remain the soul of this transformation. The best AI systems will not replace educators—they will empower them to do what technology cannot: inspire imagination, nurture resilience, and build human connection. In classrooms of the future, teachers will act as *learning architects* and *emotional guides*, curating AI tools that adapt to each student while fostering collaboration, empathy, and social growth. The human role in education will evolve, not vanish.

AI will also redefine **global collaboration in learning**. Through real-time translation, virtual classrooms, and cross-cultural data sharing, students from different nations will learn together without language or geographic barriers. Imagine a child in Ghana and another in Finland co-creating a climate change project, guided by an AI system that translates, mentors, and tracks progress seamlessly. Such experiences not only expand intellectual horizons but deepen cultural empathy—reminding us that intelligence, whether natural or artificial, is most powerful when it connects rather than divides.

However, as AI grows more capable, **the moral dimension of teaching** becomes even more critical. Educators must model ethical decision-making, transparency, and compassion. This means discussing the consequences of AI openly with students—its risks as well as its rewards. Students should learn to question algorithms, identify bias, and understand that technology carries the values of its creators. The classroom of tomorrow will not only teach code—it will teach *conscience.*

Finally, the future of AI in education is not about machines taking over—it is about *machines taking part.* AI will handle the repetitive, analytical, and administrative aspects of education, while humans will focus on imagination, mentorship, and wisdom. The schools that thrive in the coming decades will be those that achieve this balance: technologically advanced yet profoundly human-centered.

In this vision, education is no longer a one-way transmission of knowledge but a dynamic, lifelong dialogue between humans and their intelligent creations. It is a world where data informs decisions but empathy guides them—where automation increases access but never replaces care. The challenge ahead is not just to design smarter systems, but to nurture wiser humans who use them. The real future of AI in education, therefore, is not artificial—it is deeply, beautifully human.

"The Human Code"

When Principal Elena Torres walked through the halls of Horizon Academy, the hum of technology was everywhere. Robots delivered books between classrooms. Smartboards translated lessons into six languages in real time. Every student had a personal AI tutor that tracked progress and suggested enrichment activities. On paper, it was the most advanced school in the state—yet something felt missing. Teachers complained of burnout from constant data monitoring. Students performed well on tests but seemed disengaged from one another. "We've built the future," Elena thought, "but where is the heart?"

One afternoon, she sat with a student named Mira, who had perfect grades but little joy in learning. "I just follow what my AI tells me to do," Mira admitted. "It's efficient, but it doesn't feel like me." That conversation stayed with Elena. The next day, she gathered her staff and posed a challenge: "We've taught our students how to work with AI. Now we need to teach them how to *feel* with it."

Together, they launched a pilot program called **The Human Code**—a project designed to reintroduce empathy, ethics, and creativity into an AI-driven school. Students began using their AI systems not just to complete tasks but to explore human questions: What does fairness mean? How does empathy shape innovation? Can machines understand art, emotion, or humor? Each week, teachers encouraged them to debate ethical scenarios, collaborate on creative projects, and even design their own "values algorithms." The results were surprising. A group of seventh graders programmed their AI tutors to ask reflective questions like "How did you feel about today's lesson?" or "What would make you proud of your work?" Another team built an app that matched students from different cultures for storytelling sessions guided by real-time translation. Slowly, laughter and curiosity began returning to the classrooms.

Teachers, too, rediscovered their purpose. Freed from administrative overload by AI automation, they spent more time mentoring, listening, and connecting. The school's walls, once filled with screens of charts and analytics, began displaying student art, poetry, and projects about compassion. One poster read: **"Artificial Intelligence can think fast—but kindness thinks deep."**

Months later, during a district visit, education officials praised Horizon Academy's performance metrics. But what caught their attention wasn't the data—it was the atmosphere. Students spoke confidently about ethics, teamwork, and creativity. "Your students sound...human," one official said, almost in disbelief. Elena smiled. "That's our goal."

The school's transformation soon made headlines. Reporters dubbed Horizon "the empathy-powered school." Parents noticed their children discussing moral dilemmas at dinner, questioning not only how things work but *why*. Even the AI systems evolved—trained through thousands of student interactions to recognize gratitude, humor, and empathy as indicators of success. The machines, it seemed, were learning humanity too.

On the final day of the year, the graduating class presented their capstone project: a manifesto titled *"The Human Code."* It began with a simple declaration: **"We use AI not to replace thinking, but to deepen it. We build technology not to outsmart humanity, but to understand it better."**

When Elena read those words aloud, she felt tears in her eyes. She looked around at her students—smiling, curious, alive—and realized that the future she once feared had become something far greater than she imagined. The machines had not stolen education's soul. They had helped uncover it.

That evening, as the sun set over Horizon Academy, Elena walked past the mural the students had painted by hand. It showed a human and a robot sitting side by side, reading the same book. Underneath, a line in bold letters read: **"The**

future of learning is not artificial. It's beautifully human."

And for the first time, Elena believed it.

Epilogue

Teaching in the Age of Intelligence

As we stand at the intersection of human intelligence and artificial intelligence, education finds itself facing the greatest transformation since the invention of the printing press. For centuries, teachers have been the architects of civilization—builders of knowledge, character, and progress. Now, as algorithms and neural networks join the learning process, the role of the educator has not diminished—it has evolved. This evolution is not about surrendering control to machines; it's about reclaiming the essence of what it means to teach in a world that learns faster than ever before.

Artificial Intelligence has proven it can grade, translate, analyze, and even explain. But what it cannot do is care. It cannot replace the warmth in a teacher's encouragement, the intuition that senses a student's hidden potential, or the compassion that sees ability where others see struggle. The future of education belongs not to those who resist technology, nor to those who blindly depend on it—but to those who learn to lead it with empathy, wisdom, and courage.

This book has traced AI's path from classroom personalization to district-wide decision-making. We've seen how algorithms can adapt lessons, predict outcomes, and empower students who once felt unseen. We've watched teachers rediscover joy through intelligent coaching, and students find their voices through tools that listen without judgment. Every story, every system, every innovation points to the same truth: **AI's greatest achievement in education is not automation—it's amplification.**

Education has always been about transformation—of minds, of possibilities, of entire societies. AI merely accelerates that transformation, creating a future where learning never stops. Imagine a world where every learner has a tutor that understands their rhythm, every teacher has an assistant who amplifies their strengths, and every leader makes decisions guided by truth, not guesswork. That world is not decades away—it is already being built.

Yet progress must walk hand in hand with principles. The educators of tomorrow must be not only technologically skilled but ethically grounded. They must teach students not just how to use AI, but how to question it, challenge it, and shape it responsibly. The ultimate goal is not to produce perfect test scores or flawless automation—it's to cultivate critical thinkers, innovators, and compassionate citizens who understand the value of both data and dignity.

To every teacher, trainer, and leader reading this: you are not being replaced. You are being redefined. You are the bridge between logic and love, between information and imagination. The classroom has no walls anymore—it extends to every screen, every conversation, every curious mind. The teacher's role is no longer to know everything but to guide learners toward discovering everything.

The next chapter of education will not be written by machines. It will be written by *humans who choose to teach in partnership with them.* And when we look back on this moment, years from now, we won't see a divide between human and artificial intelligence—we'll see a collaboration that made learning more human than it's ever been.

www.ingramcontent.com/pod-product-compliance
Lightning Source LLC
LaVergne TN
LVHW020236210926
848481LV00016B/2340
9798295409813